All the People Are Pregnant

Also by Andrew DuBois

Start to Figure: Fugitive Essays, Selected Reviews
He We Her/I Am White
The Anthology of Rap (co-edited with Adam Bradley)
Ashbery's Forms of Attention
Close Reading: The Reader (co-edited with Frank Lentricchia)

All the People Are Pregnant

Andrew DuBois

icehouse poetry
an imprint of Goose Lane Editions

Copyright © 2021 by Andrew DuBois.

All rights reserved. No part of this work may be reproduced or used in any form or by any means, electronic or mechanical, including photocopying, recording, or any retrieval system, without the prior written permission of the publisher or a licence from the Canadian Copyright Licensing Agency (Access Copyright). To contact Access Copyright, visit accesscopyright.ca or call 1-800-893-5777.

Edited by Katie Fewster-Yan.
Cover and page design by Julie Scriver.
Cover illustration by donatas1205, 123rf.com, image ID 1770512.
Printed in Canada by Coach House Printing.
10 9 8 7 6 5 4 3 2 1

Library and Archives Canada Cataloguing in Publication

Title: All the people are pregnant / Andrew DuBois.
Names: DuBois, Andrew (Andrew Lee), author.
Identifiers: Canadiana 20200311204 | ISBN 9781773101804 (softcover)
Subjects: LCGFT: Poetry.
Classification: LCC PS8607.U26 A79 2021 | DDC C811/.6—dc23

Some of these poems first appeared in *The Archive*, *Dispatches from the Poetry Wars*, *echolocation*, *The Lights Are Out*, *South Atlantic Quarterly*, and *White Wall Review*.

Goose Lane Editions acknowledges the generous financial support of the Government of Canada, the Canada Council for the Arts, and the Province of New Brunswick.

Goose Lane Editions
500 Beaverbrook Court, Suite 330
Fredericton, New Brunswick
CANADA E3B 5X4
gooselane.com

*To
Josh May
and
Rachel Daley*

Contents

I.

All the People Are Pregnant   11
North and South but in German   14
The Battle of Sulfur Creek Trestle   15
Coffin of Sticks   17
Infidels over the Hills   18
Rules for and Secrets About   20
Hanalei   21

II.

Partners   25
The Puppet Museum   26
Grease Fantasy   27
Mr. and Mrs. Refusal   28
And and Any Love   29
Bent Fabric   31
Tulip Hysteria Coordinating   32
Poinciana   34

III.

I am come to you as an alien.   37
Fear Eats the Soul   38
Blood for Wizard Oil   39
Campaign Confetti   40
Clown Condom   42
Genie fur   44

Blind Blake   45
Landscape with Amorous Couple   46
Yellow Tulips   47
Yellow Bird   48
The Hole of Harm and Moaning   49
Sublunary Moon   50
Lightning Bulb   51

IV.

Song   55
Studies in Neurobiology   56
The Real Morning (after Frances Farmer)   61
Fictional Residency   67
Bellcore   71

I.

All the People Are Pregnant

Hit parade of slummery floats down these
    slummy memories of streets—
Refuse collected by accident resting blown,
    or having been thrown angry
From a last ditch, against an effort
    of a building erected by proximity
To eternity being zoned out of repression,
    into dilapidation, crumbling, wafer-
Boarded over every way to see, and the taking
    away of everything seen, as if
Too far from to partake of living, or maybe
    dying coming close to the nose like a book
Listing all the unliving by tallow light, shaking
    the spine alphabetically, until you get
Near the name where your eyes give out,
    finally, and that being the most important name;
Enlisting everyone you've ever unknown to hold
    the wires of the balloons, to keep these full
Cartoons from flying off like clean streets
    we had a filthy handle on.
Because it will take people places, remem-
    bering; to places, like streets, and from
Places, like huge parade cartoon balloons
    which are crying out for flight,
Webbing minus feet, wing, or direction,
    difference or purpose. The point is escape,
Whether undesired of age or lost attention,
    cultivated maybe in the case of the cables
Cutting the hands, therein the letting go.

And to say who this is for is hard as a bottle
    is hard before you break it, spilling
Our last shot at retrieval, the first dozen
    for forgetting why we need to forget
To begin with, the thirteenth to hit
    the happy point and that wasn't it.
You were the greatest queen of England once,
    surrounding an island surrounded—
By a vivid fear of fluidity, by
    insistence openness forced.
Methinks I am a puppet unretired, and this
    desiring do forestall to hymn.
The hottest fires are purple as a bruise,
    though violet fires do burn themselves out soon.

A little death, all right, and numbers to be
    remembered, caught in the web that's
Conflating too much. Still, a digit was lost
    in the stable—a seven,
So there was never any sense of completion;
    an elaborate Gallic irony,
Centered round concepts of sundering
    middles—a done deal—and a place,
A stable where the seven was spilled with
    the trough, instigating thy fearful
Instability. The men with torches frightened
    your horses, they were looking for the dark.
It was nowhere where they thrust their
    torches; throw your arms around
The necks of horses.

And verses and knuckles, small scratches
    on the knuckles, sucking all day,

Vampiric desiring, a noble mobility from
    wall to painted wall, painted with
Lichens and old money from cotton,
    dropping the weevilled boll.
We lost some things along the way,
    and when we found them again
They were very different things. Tinges
    of urge grew into clutchery,
Then setting a table, the placemat torn,
    everything dead like cells
Or especially even fingernails shorn and
    that's the thing you call beautiful,
The dead part. Well maybe it draws me
    livid, this offer of African violets,
A neck bouquet, an April lozenge. It's not
    that I'm shallow, I'm hollow, after every
Last call one feels empty, drained as a bucket
    of peaches.

All the people are pregnant here, they
    are full of something—but what
They can't say, or how it got there
    they can't say or can't imagine.
Was it magic? The wand doesn't work
    without religion, but I can pull
A rabbit out for slaughter. I tried to write
    them in love with me, but all I could
Write was a story—called "Breathless,"
    beginning, "The ice cubes were
Horribly dusty, the room filled with the
    smoke of indifference. She touched
His neck, but she was lying. 'Don't hold
    your breath,' the queen said to
Her subject. 'With me, there's no tomorrow.'"

North and South but in German

This is a cursed poem, Tiamat split
    into rivers
        the sun a pregnant letter.
This is now a callus or wax
the sun a broken chalice.

Broken pleasure yester-
day
a new language for thieves
who can't laugh in Russian translation
tee-he-he through an overcoat
false full of mortar.

Take brick from a stable kiln
to orbit
strain on the door
a flag unfurled, a silver tongue
made slow
the region—the cold face—no war
is predetermined.
We'll speak.
The eyes of God ship the words up
North, it's south but in German.

The Battle of Sulfur Creek Trestle

          I.

There was hunger and thirst.
The barrels had been dumped
upstream. Fire spoke to conductors,
saying, "Stop. Turn your train around.
The bridge and cross-ties are burned,
only the rails are left floating."

There was no rain with the thunder
and it was too late even if there was.
But it is hard to take a hill when
there are trenches and reasons.

And then it was built back in stone,
a union from the breach, for trains.
Stronger, it was said, but also that
at night you could see dark light
through the tunnel, that was a ghost.

          II.

This is the place my father built
his house. There had been crops
up here, well fertilized.

I was loading firewood when
the man said, "Do you know what
you people have done here?"
Worked up to this place. So I said

you from here and where'd you get
that jacket and is that your name.

"Army surplus."
I know you I said.
"There are ghosts
down there," he said.

Naw I said that's just
a water station with
a light set up by the
Tennessee Valley Authority.

Coffin of Sticks

This here's just a old
Coffin full of sticks
A box been flagged and dusted
With glistering grains of sand

Infidels over the Hills

Somebody did this, or some poor soul. Patrols roll by,
    Suspects gather flowers from fields of vision.
I love it when they lay down grids where no grids are,
    They once did that on this space too. No longer.
How cruel and unusual, to force them to find their demise:
    Yes, we left it there, but that's why we left it.
And thus the smoking gun recovered in, say,
    Square A3 snaps into fantasy ordered, a great
Groove in time and time's conspiratorial movement,
    So even if the wind erased the winding smoke
—it did—that sidearm is loaded with significance
    In a different way than if the lieutenant says,
"Hell, looks like he dumped it near the stump."

There's an urge to theory. There are roofers. There in
    The wilderness, the woods, the hackers of tree-
Trunks speaking intimately of forestry. It was an instrument
    I played and played well (never apologize) although
To be honest, well frankly, the whole thing seems to have soured.
    Kept running into floss strung from tree to tree like
Spiderwebs—what with the other stuff in between,
    That forest was a long-drawn continuum of animal contact.

    And death and people dying: it forces order in the chaos
That it forces. A square in the grid, a dot on the line. Don't be fooled,
    It only subtracts, even the things it adds take away.
This jacket I wore while smoking—you'll always remember where
    I threw it down, square D6, and always hold it against me.
Don't. You should give me consolation. Vodka, tonic, lime.
    Of course, it all comes back like pollution—the medicinal kiss.
We have tattoos: a flower, yours; mine, a flaming sword
    With the legend "Trust your enemies, fear your friends.

Nothing is easy apart from a few million things and what we make hard
On ourselves. You can't have him or her. There is a glow,
A burning from a campfire so old no records were destroyed."
And what does that prove? It carries over—
There was once a great voluptuary that will never not cry at night again.

These shovels, they are the devil. Comparatively a pinprick
Interrogation. "Suspected" gathers flower. Searching for land,
I was lost, you were more so, I thought you had drowned.
It is never exhausted. It's there, it's there, we'll always find
New ways to hurt and places. Some say the safe estate is the state that's
Left untroubled. Over the crest of the hills come legions—
Men, women, perhaps someday a child. One wears a shroud,
Another a shape. Their cries are growing more abstract.

We are huddled in a little church, dilapidated, the roof unbuilt,
The walls fall down. You hold me against your wishes. They are
Upon us now—horrible, loud, kaleidoscopic: our history.
Mystified. Outrageous. Now biting my ear—expansion, destiny—
Whispering three little words: *location location location.*

Rules for and Secrets About

It is "rumors of ghosts chained to ghosts"
   (set yourself on fire)
   all tide and gasoline;
   not butterflies but birds that eat their young.
   Rotary dial a pulse and shut your mouth;
   this is numbers and napalm,
   anniversaries
   (to suck you out)
   to suck out the oxygen from the skin of time.
It is happy and a happy lie and la-di-da,
   defining terms, with wine
   (soft in the mouth to say if it is anything
   it is two swans whispering).

Hanalei

Our Golden Age of pigtails. This crash time has seconds
    added to years which we all recognize as days,
do we not, the final unit—a hundred years a kiss.
    Perhaps you could feel a different way, tie the bow
in a dove knot or paint the candles with wax
    from the finger piano which we hardly play at all.
What is left is a woman, a man, trees and bricks and people
    mentioning Spain as if it were still there after all of this.
But something is amiss, and if that seems gratuitous
    you should see the sex, write a poem for every lover
and write a multitude of poems, excessive and tedious.
    Birds don't fly with less regularity, there's
the Protestant notion of ravens where the molting breeds disease.
    It's a thing you've disregarded, spurred on by a diet of knots,
houses of rum and wormwood where discussions of fusion
    generate cold fusion, cold sores, cold orthodoxy
slow with age like a split lip on a stained bystander.
    So what if I left language by the pier. Metaphor's a raft,
it was an island once, though even then the sand
    became pearls, natives recall oysters and swine,
overhead projections leaving the tropics seeming Greenland, not
    Iceland, not the Canaries, either, named for dogs, not canaries,
either. If this is how we know each other, how do we
    know each other? *Trompe le monde*, webs and correlation,
ultra-sticky; sensational murders where one can, one cannot survive.
    When the wind is low you mostly say things like
"What's the use in stories?" and I have to agree until
    five minutes later you tell of a city of women
shorn of hair and dying. "The city or the women," I ask.
    "See, that's the trouble with stories," you say, hands like gulls
on crippled walls, flightless and the worse for it
    because uncontained, no boundaries erects a boundary

against itself, like lovers free to roam Europe using bad French,
    or words unconstrained that could say something
but anything at all will do. What map is this, a country
    undiscovered slowly. "Untrammel thyself!"
Call in the dogs, the mongeese, the orders. Coordinate the carpet
    bombs, they could paint the bridge with napalm
if the papers were in order. Whose feather is this?
    Let's pretend we're elderly, okay, we're just about dead so don't
make a sound. I'm tired of thinking you're robotic, angelic.
    Wherever there are horses that's where we'll be,
open spaces dirty and clean, scalps removed with scalpels,
    a certain efficiency there, add an elevated train,
and in the question posed softly over Kansas plum wine,
    "Married or alone?" "Both," she said writhing,
drawing lines at caring or referring to the places we have been.
    There are things that we don't need to know,
dragons and such, where they come from.
    Is there a mathematician in the house? Could you
make some calculations—we'll invade Amsterdam and New
    Amsterdam, use the word "bifurcate," introduce birds
that can run. It always cracks me up. I have no desire for
    children or glamour, but who can really say.

The shadows made sevens. You were gone, practicing.
    I didn't think to call you, there were heavenly sirens
and the guns were firing crazily, five thousand rounds a minute,
    each fifth round a flare like a cycle, love, a hundred years.
Did anyone notice the silence? I can half-relate. There is always
    the unfulfilled desire to speak, to say something, anything
new, not necessarily to say, "There is a boy who knows this country
    well but will never know it first." A hard sickness to learn,
not the end of the world, just the century. There is always
    the wet reflection.

II.

Partners

"The putrefaction of unspoken obscenities issuing from that tomb of flesh, devoid of any magnetism, chilled my powdered skin."
—Mina Loy

Craven apes.
Simian henchmen.
Haters who love to spit
In each other's faces.

Cry next day, abused babies.
Lucky to be alive, though;
Mostly we play dead.
I smack your head.

You slap back, evolving
Claws. We kiss.
Two tongues
Tore out.

Clutching,
Silent, frantic apes.
Cold mates.
Partners in mime.

The Puppet Museum

Take a nap in the car, the shadows, and the sun.
It is cold outside but today it is warm in the car.

Puppets tell us much about ourselves, like how long to wait.
They mimic our wooden behavior, and when their strings are released,
    inert with life, they mimic sleep.

We pulled up to a vast museum.
We stepped inside the empty barn.

You were hurt but I wouldn't console you for the lack of puppets there.
Our last kept promise was never to touch, I mean, never to let puppets
    touch our lives again.

Grease Fantasy

I rose from the cot,
Turned to my cell door.
"You crazy damn fool," I shouted,
Keys unlocking my door.

"Pipe down, I want your attention."
I thumbed my nose, ignored.
"Come on back here," I shouted.
"Come on, let's have some more!"

She said, "You'll get no treatment here.
You'll pick up the can and spoon,
Then crawl down the hall on your hands
And knees to grovel before the cart."

Out of the cell she puffed.
I slumped back on the cot.
To accept defeat was vile.
"Could I have some more?"
I begged in my cell, "I've been
Hungry for quite a while."

She turned and leaned her head.
"I scraped the bottom myself,"
She said. "Sweet things make things
Go better." She walked back in—

Residue of candy
In her mouth, pink
Letter "A" embroidered
On her sweater.

Mr. and Mrs. Refusal

"I refuse all the time. I refuse you. Who says I haven't wanted you?"
—Henri-Pierre Roché, *Victor*

Lives at times degenerate into victory competitions.
One wins by being defeated, by proving to another
Merely being there together is a dull catastrophe.
Try outright to win and you lose. To win, use insinuation,
Sprezzatura, lamentation; feign shudders in another's presence passing by.

Mostly, though, to keep from losing you just have to keep refusing.
Refuse to console, to listen or to ask, to bury petty hates,
To drop deceits and to admit to having falsified defeats.
Refuse to whistle, clean, have fun, or talk,
To think out loud, leave bed, go down the Old Ox Road.
(Try touching after that: cold apprehension obtains.)

I've worshipped
With people with imploding
Hearts, like those brittle spider-balls full of empty air
Under the trees at church. Righteousness
Burned them dry and then—

I appreciate acts of control like theirs, or like real punk rock
Or being a Navy Seal. But it rubs raw my better nature,
Saying no out of fear, being mean. I hereby relinquish control.
But I'll be honest, I can't do it, so you'll have to do it first.

And and Any Love

You're sensational and I wouldn't trade you
For any of the products in those windows,
Said And, and—what, said Any Love.
There were scaffolds outside the facade
Of their hearts. They were getting paint jobs:
Planks alongside canals, joists astride slim houses
With tall, narrow windows with jutting hooks atop.

Well, said Any Love, you think
There's not a red curtain drawn
In my heart, said smiling some.
No takers, said And, well knowing
Any Love would go like hotcakes
And that Any Love would know.

And and Any Love were unemployed.
They didn't need their jobs in the world.
Their hearts floated down the canals.

Just as boats have tops and bottoms,
And hotcakes have two sides,
And and Any Love had two sides each.

Next they needed a chimney
And kin of And said "chimley."
Any Love threw a garden party where
Folks referred to seat-rows as "blenchers."
Not unphased apart, the two
Together cut a demanding Turducken.

For Xmas And and Any Love
Exchangéd presents.
Any Love gave And

A watch and chain or fob,
Got with cash that could be parted with.
And gave Any Love a lovely hat,
To cover lovely hair,
On special days,
A bargain.

When times got tough
They had those scaffolds,
That watch that never faltered,
Ditto fob, hat, and hair.

There was rain for And and Any Love.
They always made it through the rain, however.
The rain weren't too unpleasant
Where them two were at, anyways.
Then the sunshine on the canals, on the windows
On the narrow, hook-prowed houses with red,
Green, orange, yellow paintjobs, with pastel
Highlights, and for every junkie,
A bike.

Bent Fabric

You, you sound you take me back to the time to the time that
    we

You, you era of drapes and painted panels good for the heart
    that we

You, you see the folds pile up in angles and kind of like
    shards that we

You, you that study robes beneath the crucifix those worried
    lines that we

You, you in mystic states in mystical robes in saintlihood
    divest yourself that we

You, you crouched down by bent fabric counting folds
    counting times that we

Tulip Hysteria Coordinating

"One only has: for female *the public urinal and one* lives *by it."*
—Marcel Duchamp

I only have a hole
    my mouth
I want to be a mother
    between my lips
you cram
    my throat
you choke me
    so soothe me

I fall to my forearms
    from my knees
I gag then retch
    in the urine
you laugh
    "you taste yourself"

I love you
    don't be cold
I walk on my knees
    open my mouth
you are all
    so warm

I can't hold
    so much
you have all
    been drinking
you sigh to let it out
    gushing in my eyes

"open your eyes"
        in my eyes
they let me
        urinate

Poinciana

Poinciana, I loved living in her
Who made me feel like a million in one
She grew bigger every day
Until she filled my mind
She filled the rest
My conscience broke, violated
But my heart said deserved
I gave in and began
To relax, bombs in the head
And I began to know death
And remorse when I heard
Your name, Poinciana, fear,
Waning pride, a native son, but
You Dame Champ, the one
Who win.

III.

I am come to you as an alien.

I am sorry that my fault have make much trouble to you.

I too lay my threadbare heart to you.

I spin the wheel of the Future of Luck.

Like the child on the shore I pick up the cobble and find the whole sea.

—

I dream to worry in you since a little thing.

Though quite honesty, I am a little jealousy.

I dream to inside your pink eastern bones.

I remain your green light.

Fear Eats the Soul

An auslander here is called alien
Only one without misshapen body
Love is a saving decision
A smoke every night on the bed
What does the auslander see
Smudges of grease on the face
Mechanical auslander
A serial name
O auslander come from the cold
Young will soon be old
The fear of fear eat soul
The soul of fear eat you

Blood for Wizard Oil

R and D come up with new approach
    Engine run with red red blood
The civilized woman and man now turn
    In their hour of desperate need to the vampire
If we cannot be good we gonna be careful
    The earth is happy now but now me watch me neck
This sharp fang bunch try every day to siphon there

We gonna run out of blood like we just bout run out of wizard oil
    Then them that's got then them gets more
Them who's got like barrels of blood piled up
    Rusty barrels w/ numbers & names wrote up in chalk
R and D don't know them don't anticipate
    That blood don't have that special magic though
That stuff too common that stuff don't got that evil magic power

See you see it ain't consistent like good diesel or kerosene evil
    Blood ain't no equation function
Wizard oil encompass what all
    We call that good clean blood
Which don't run things long
    And it don't even
Make us strong

Campaign Confetti

1.

Did I ever tell you the one about the two
    vultures who were plucking each other?

2.

The reproduction of an experiment
    with identical outcomes.
a CopGod   law and order
H-bomb   candidate

3.

The policeman wouldn't listen
And was buried this morning:
    his approach to how models
                         are used

4.

Wine or beer   Both   vice versa
Campaign   The platform
Sings   *shrilly*   Watch
    wince
                         wheels or gyres

5.

Don't give rope
      the coming out
Watch my mouth
      my twin has been
Say hoot owl
      claimed (a positioning
      of identity as contingent)

    hair, glasses
        to try to say

    well-worn   so plainly

        techniques

Clown Condom

Straight from the shores of Lake Champlain

    tens of thousands, hundreds of thousands of thousands

computed, a cloud dis-
chargéd, a veritable Milky Way,
as Stendhal thought of love

    of ships come in

a charnel house (?) of possible clowns
of bad bad clowns, redundantly sad
of piratical clowns, reciting it into my head
a discarded (?) poem about a balloon (?)

    all about

              bicycles then balloons
* * *

"blow up, blow up"

an undone used-up crêpe-paper poem
a show from Chicago, ping-pong balls in pails (?)
bouncing balls in the morning
        then, in the night, helmets for a mouse

* * *

the lowest form of wit, the clown

    (domestic clowns,
        not fancy foreign clowns)

we were talking about balloons,
of pails, bent balloons and mask,
of untouched cymbal,
puppets, a tambourine,
a flying disc, some
dumb chumps,
a multi-instru-
mentalist

                    seltzer versus chicken

* * *

"Ahoy, I wax thee wroth"
This lake is full of ruins

    of

nandu, nandu, nandu

    oh

I'm um, um, um, um, I'm

sorry I never found my way
sorry I didn't eat your eggs
so the hell with all, the hell

    with all

these clowns and their dis-
carded, speckled, cherry-colored condoms.

Genie fur

won't be genteel genie fur
momma say gourd a skull
she done sin sin a city bore
hard to thank about that gull

climb a fork you hole yes?
split chew ought a dim chains
climb a sack on gnat-ass
shore you who ain't no queens

genie fur grown a-cry
genie fur is a-goin in-oh in-oh
grown a-orphan is a-door
show you orphan or for shore

you done done collared mary
bleach eye swear eye black
split chew spit chew spit chew spit
make you whole and round

and word my crown

Blind Blake

Blake was blinded in an eye
    For brawling with a boy,
Blake was blinded in an eye,
        An eye, for brawling;

But some words had been exchanged
    And the circumstance arranged
        For the boy and Blake
            To answer every challenge.

Landscape with Amorous Couple

Peasants painted over
Now restored, man with
His hand on her breast.

Yellow Tulips

Yellow tulips so wide open they're about to fold back
on their own self, touch your own neck with the back
of your own right hand, where bottoms look like onions
in the bowl. Where did they come from? It's snowing
outside in the middle of March. One imagines where
they come from. One was only there last summer, safe
in oneself, arranging daily tulips, no snow, never will.

Yellow Bird

You little bird
Tell me to call you a songbird
You shine your little coat
Which we mop up
After we despoil it
Bird who screams and skitters
As a caged and tortured bird
A yellow bird in a rusty cage
A bookish hateful hand
Darts in to grab the bird
It gets the yellow bird
And squeezes out its song:
"If the birds up in the trees can be free
Then why the chirp can't we?"

The Hole of Harm and Moaning

In Washington did Kubla Khan
Decree his obelisk shaft poke through
The mall and the mail via postcards,
And so it was for perpetuity.

The mosquitoes were thick with gunk.
The mice, the swine, the imported hogs
Snooted and rooted against the dirty
Assholes of all the others.

The vista was flat and shallow,
Peppered with herds.
Underneath the shallow was
The very deep.

Its immutability was interrupted.

Sublunary Moon

Shine your question, moon that glows:
"Have you always carried your own death within you?"

I figure so, but it never dawned on me to offer you something.
If you needed placating after all, I didn't mean to eclipse you.

Lightning Bulb

Does a bear not get fat in the winter? But is man not a kind of a bear?

Sanguine his eyes. He can see with his claws.

Some sharp property. Some unpleasant shifting.

Does a bear not get fat in the winter? And we deduce . . .

No things no think nor think in things, a summary of the character of the thing.

He slumbers up from out some hole, they little bitty lightnings up the thing.

He breathe and look from one to one, he nose it out, he flare the thing,

He swat a little bit. He go back down. It start to rain.

IV.

Song

My bent-backwards neck
Is tired of the sky
Yet the ground offers
No consolation

An azure affront
To the brown of my eye
And the ground offers
No consolation

Dark inclemency
Wearies me further
Bright sun and soft breeze
Mock me further

The mutable weather
Embodies my loss
The ground
Is not less changing

Now falls the rain
Dispassionate rain
Now lukewarm rays
On expanses of dirt

On excuses for days
Beneath the sky
Where the ground offers
No consolation

Studies in Neurobiology

"The account which follows will be concerned chiefly with the reciprocal connections which exist between the hypothalamus and the gyrus cinguli and hippocampus. Its chief purpose is to point out that these connections may mediate by means of the cortical circuit the important function commonly called emotion."
—James W. Papez, MD, "A Proposed Mechanism of Emotion"

sleep is not a bank—or even not a kiss
for when the pig is unalive

salt these wounds with rusted shears
this pig must be a little sheep

what are broken must be teeth
fears or snakes are writhing in this vault

life is when we trick the dead
disbelief is what is cut

strychnine spikes invite the driven charge
bed it down then take the knife

EEG will prove to you that you are only real
barge is driven impulse (prick-

ing pain is localized)
feel this—this is where it says "you hurt me"

drop electrodes on this coiléd spot
synchronized glass on a diamond ring

you say "at this point I am called asleep
not when stimulation makes / when makes / high voltage stop

low fast-voltage called a wake
deep inside this self is nothing new

it is / it is / over" done
"make / thalamic make / the waves roll slow

brain stem split—lemniscus for the fall
sun is / over sun is / over" quit

thunderhead inside the brutal skull
wall of skull surround the brittle rain

storm is stress and called deep thought
"pull that reading, doc, and keep the subject under"

never what is mine is mine
ought to know desire is only impulse fit to form

not in this equation ever know
sine : cosine : mathematical : lever

magnify synapses with a glass
show "insane" is information clot

you say "the magnifying glass we own is gold
pass the magic dime to pacify

with bloody reeds we made a dragonfly with wings
sold on a string / on a / spoke with a few"

dark waves of the brain and new muse—she
sings laments for autonomy, taking the Fifth

"sin not," she maintains while lifting her woolen hat
"be not soul / electricity / full remain stark"

oh those whose hands are
that which shed the winter skin

turn us over once again to hateful gods
bar this circuit from the house where spirits flow

stares are long but blank—machines are faulty
rods probe—sleep is not a bank—memories burn

these dreams will not sustain investment
salty water buoys no one up in chairs

* *

"Hall... has recently proposed the dichotomy of pain and suffering; suffering can be experienced without pain, and pain may not involve suffering, unless severe and presented under conditions arousing anxiety or other emotional disturbance."
—George H. Bishop, PhD, "The Relation between Nerve Fiber Size and Sensory Modality: Phylogenetic Implications of the Afferent Innervation of Cortex"

there are two tongues in this beast
one mouth, or even two mouths—

this mouth is the house that eats
the flesh or the flesh itself

from this mouth which speaks are
the teeth, each tooth

a house in the city of the dead
each mouth a city unto itself

this city a house of the flesh
all dead flesh a mouth

this mouth secures all teeth buried under
dirt floors in the houses of saints

on the seventh day Anubis, god
of magnification, decrees over ouzo

"all mosaic made from local stone" stop
"couples rub dry inside the door" stop

"cut tesserae in cubes" stop "color must be local"
stop "everything in two" stop—thus

arousal here, of what—the tense is pleasure
perfect pleasure pathway

untranslatable word, loosely joy,
bliss, the envelope text

all shut in two and come
unglued, bartered open

a tongue for a tooth—
lover, bodycup, pour me in

for pain   I am the last
true cannibal worth my weight in salt

* *

"The discussion relates to subcortical activities which are common to fishes and men."
—C. Judson Herrick, "The Functions of the Olfactory Parts of the Cerebral Cortex"

where stare is cold resolve
is bold: grey eye, marksman;

blue eye, blessed. the child's eye
wavers not from the back of the pew.

at a distance: the sweetgum cuts
the eye; scraping rust from darting

eye. shiny things, things that move.
thrash around about then dangle.

deep focus through muddy water.
dark stench of bottled emulsion.

cadaverous. best taken with wine.
travels in schools. covered in scales.

The Real Morning (after Frances Farmer)

I.

The real morning is,
as it were, a place
never heard; still,
the place lies.

II.

For years the years past deteriorated—only grief twisting memory from the comfort of isolation contributed to the beginning of a sentence.

III.

For nearly a year a crumbling house was found to be completely without funds. Curiously, M-O-N-E-Y and silence hung around in uneven scallops, deliberately warned against—but like curling smoke—in the first case ("Don't use that word!") and hung scared as a pretense (a towel draped over a spike nail carelessly driven into plaster) in the second. The yellow walls that needed washing and the porch locked into disrepair were always a big secret.

The middle of the night did it before and again would do it, but new actors were needed. Maybe ("A good role. A real challenge.") cast Cary Grant. It wouldn't hurt, that's for sure. A nice man (Cary Grant) knows what to do with it (the house); but, intent on being Cary Grant playing Grant, an actor is the toast of New York, not a designing harlot. Honest Hollywood distortion instead of Sunnybrook safely tucked into a chastity belt. So the actor remained an ingenious scheme, nothing more.

Anxiety lay just below the surface. The house kept money chirping by reminding itself, with its silence, of its fermenting lack. A strange paradoxical escape hatch preserved, in contradiction, some degree of the character of this "home," such as it was—an aggravation, a rundown country musty from the darkness or the morning, a blind man halting and mumbled; but filled with old fire and making no attempt to hide the fact that the sting was raw but defiantly and continually unremembered.

IV.

An armless wooden chair was bolted to the floor. Around the room a heavy-jowled man seemed detached. Other people were wandering around the room like gnomes—chattering, pleading. Occasionally order would bang against the wire-covered peephole, "Shut up in there! Shut up, or I'll take the belt to you!"

 Brought on, it stuck out like a broken knuckle. A toothless old man hopped up and down in front of the young. The tight circle, the blue worms, the tight knot had huddled quietly until they whipped the air with them. They then twisted free.

 "Get that crazy out of here!"
 "Goddamned motherfuckers!"

 A pale-skin swung his towel like a branding iron. Blood spurted, a head shattered.

 "You filthy son of a bitch!"
 "You lousy son of a bitch!"

 He drew back the towel again. "I'll show you who's a motherfucker."

 At that moment he stepped out unceremoniously. The room was still stained, by silence spraddled and exposed. A constricted spasm of despair rolled in from far off. The room was localizing the pain that racked it raw.

* * *

The dim corridor stopped before a door with the word ISOLATION stenciled across its face.

To maneuver was work.

"You can go now, you can write on this."

A yellow pad and a stub of pencil, pad and pencil.

Its influence was asylum and autograph.

It was its own physician, surrounded by weird creatures.

It was the caged and the keeper.

It was at their disposal but would never submit.

So paper the universe proving it.

Terms cannot prevent the mind from functioning, though memory is *almost* halted.

Fineries added to miseries are whatever label is attached.

The words are inside the walls.

"I can't imagine."

A contributor might say, "Guess who they brought in today?"

"Guess who I rapped across the mouth today?"

"Guess who's gone crazy?"

Still, to think.

Still, to function.

To retaste each day of the past, finding the past revealed in the future.

Before an open crematorium.

V.

Life is many beginnings linked in mysterious chain—that is one opinion. Others discovered that night was almost every night, a part of the world not setting the world on fire or ducking in and out of the infirmary. It was conspicuous and absorbed in structure. It was also not a first.

From that there was no turning back. Writing faded quickly into a vague past. Everyone responded to the Method. The real core of the Method was reality—the worn strumpet. It had to be real, according to the standards. The Method became a moving force. Memory should have served as a stoplight, but ignored, the warning existed without benefit.

Pandemonium followed. One woman kept peering over heads in the hope of getting a closer look: *This is the real thing. This is it.*

The Group based its methods on the Method. It was imperative to belong to the Group. Scoffed at, the unreal was enraged by the deplorable conditions brought on by the people in the Group. Contact with the Group was a radical nothing openly conducting a contest, with the winner receiving an all-expense-paid round trip to anything big and easy. Some very raw whiskey couldn't attack the menace, though it never occurred to me to involve myself otherwise.

Fictional Residency

1.

This morning in this world
I thought I was God. In the
eighties I felt very electric.

I had the sensation I would
explode when some body
touched me. I was constantly

angry but I was just super.
I would take out the center
of the city in all directions.

I would always feel protected.
Between the boat and balance
it was hard to walk up stairs.

I lived in my egg and felt very
protected without feeling
that they could seize me.

I wasn't afraid anymore.
I could touch them and
they couldn't touch me.

2.

I smashed against the wall
but was unbreakable.
I started to emprison.

I discovered to think things
away you can simply forget.
I married one. We lie—

The crystal never breaks.
I must have been the prison
who could never die.

Years ago I travelled to tempt
fate. I picked out a point on
the map everywhere bigger.

I had opened every corner
of the universe. That's what
it said on the sign in the photo.

The boot took out their camera.
The boot again left the keys inside.
Imagine: I will never get out of here.

3.

In this world I was all that
the mountains in the distance
were already. And then,

Unbelievably, something extra
sort of named Napoleon was
sitting on a big silver platter.

I thought that cruelty would
live on forever and that the future
would be left on the planet.

I was raised in the former
Dutch colony. "What does
the white star mean?"

"The white star!" "The white
star are the people!" I used
the color of people.

In the end I gave up
coloring people's skin.
Today I am the star.

4.

The Sisters of the Poor feel
The Brother of the Rich. I see
their mother crossing the water.

I hear a song in my head.
It was stuck without being
called Star! I had heard

All those things—they
disappear without you
knowing. You can't know,

You have forgotten them.
I don't think about the lyrics.
It's a golden rule in my life.

I heard a giant explosion.
In all directions the world is
perfect just in front of the feet.

In a perfect world, just acting
is staged. It rips open the real world,
this thinking as if nothing had happened.

Bellcore

The start: a grisly affair. A bear of a market and we bought it.
Something
    about tendency.

We intended, I intended the sentence prior to the comma to be
    nonsensical—enough.

I thought of it as a friend. So it is, about friends. To which we shall return,
    the original endnote.

Never in a million, trillion years did I ever think, well I don't think in
    those terms. Luckily I'm in love.utterly.cathected.

The lights are on. One's reflected on the black TV, one in front of me, one
    outside. Things around the light within a certain vicinity seem
    to have a light, an area shades away. Noises upstairs are
    worrisome, the clock, some hum.

Writing. Pulling Tubes. Incident Report. Friends:
    How Many
    Of Us Have Them; Let's Be. The Anthrax Journals.

So many lessons learned, misfigured out. Too light to be a stench, burnt,
    but dank. Too cold not to be a summer brew ten seven split
    (product).
This particular bought abroad. So NY. It apparently takes your pulse on
    pause.

And it's never gonna be the same. And it's never gonna be the same!

You can almost always say stranger things have happened
    (fear inducing).
To lose all sense of the proportion of being a hunted-down outlaw.
Wiping your lips, looking around.

*Seems sometimes the things you die fighting for when you're dead they
    ain't worth fighting for anymore.*

You constitute an argument, I call you *thesis*. I am Antithesis. And to one
    who wants to be alone, the city is a thousand minarets.

Dictum: right smack in your face.

Was it true everything was an augur, had anyone said so? Don't start a
    false argument, a trail. While you're at it, I wouldn't say false. I
    mean I would, but who knows? Just to say argument, if at all.
    Necessarily breathing, inhalation argument.

The lemon-filled apartment complex.
    we?
I wanna be in a complicated trance.

A casual allusion to premeditated failure looms.
"The published city"—the bookshelf.
The casting off of the self, shedding the skin.

        shreddening

"Do not break down before them, or I will break you before them."
"Do not be dismayed at their faces, lest I confound thee before them."

We shouldn't do this anymore. We should do this more.

The argument: the landlord and his son.

No describe—on the
Other Hand
his is always really looking at
whatever it is he's looking at

The formidable tile or brick,
embossed with a city, against which
we place our pan, and rail against,
in muscle shirts, lying on
our sides on yoga mats,
eating lentil soup, prophetic tradition.

None of us are looking at

The Lanes
Won't Stop

The question is, why take it literally.
Maybe it's a thought experiment.

Remind yourself constantly:
You are not writing fiction.

Are you writing something isn't a question.

Hello, your heart must quit smoking.
The person who comes later knows more.

For literally, read seriously.

Platterstash 3-day spree
Total spent: $170

Come to find out

The perennial subject is dying as we speak, the fading rose—
and the rose
     is fading—fun.

Andrew DuBois is the author of *Ashbery's Forms of Attention*, which won the Elizabeth Agee Prize; the lyrical novella *He We Her/I Am White;* and *Start to Figure: Fugitive Essays, Selected Reviews*, a collection of more than two hundred reviews of music, film, and poetry. He also co-edited *Close Reading: The Reader* and *The Anthology of Rap*, the latter of which was named a Top Ten Book of the Year by *New York Magazine* and *The Village Voice*, called "a landmark work" by *The New York Times*, deemed an "instant classic" by Cornel West, and about which Nikki Giovanni wrote, "Much needed. Much needed."

A member of the University of Toronto's English department, DuBois, originally from Elkmont, Alabama, resides in Carbonear, Newfoundland, where he is proprietor of the Green Door Book Store. *All the People Are Pregnant* is his first collection of poetry.